YORK NOTES

Julius Caesar

William Shakespeare

Notes by Martin J. Walker

 Longman   York Press

YORK PRESS
322 Old Brompton Road, London SW5 9JH

ADDISON WESLEY LONGMAN LIMITED
Edinburgh Gate, Harlow,
Essex CM20 2JE, United Kingdom
Associated companies, branches and representatives throughout the world

First published 1998

ISBN 0-582-36834-0

Designed by Vicki Pacey, Trojan Horse, London
Phototypeset by Gem Graphics, Trenance, Mawgan Porth, Cornwall
Colour reproduction and film output by Spectrum Colour
Produced by Addison Wesley Longman China Limited, Hong Kong

CONTENTS

PREFACE

York Notes are designed to give you a broader perspective on works of literature studied at GCSE and equivalent levels. We have carried out extensive research into the needs of the modern literature student prior to publishing this new edition. Our research showed that no existing series fully met students' requirements. Rather than present a single authoritative approach, we have provided alternative viewpoints, empowering students to reach their own interpretations of the text. York Notes provide a close examination of the work and include biographical and historical background, summaries, glossaries, analyses of characters, themes, structure and language, cultural connections and literary terms.

If you look at the Contents page you will see the structure for the series. However, there's no need to read from the beginning to the end as you would with a novel, play, poem or short story. Use the Notes in the way that suits you. Our aim is to help you with your understanding of the work, not to dictate how you should learn.

York Notes are written by English teachers and examiners, with an expert knowledge of the subject. They show you how to succeed in coursework and examination assignments, guiding you through the text and offering practical advice. Questions and comments will extend, test and reinforce your knowledge. Attractive colour design and illustrations improve clarity and understanding, making these Notes easy to use and handy for quick reference.

York Notes are ideal for:
- Essay writing
- Exam preparation
- Class discussion

The author of these notes is Martin J. Walker, a Head of English, examiner and journalist. He has worked on the GCSE examinations in English and English Literature since the introduction of GCSE in 1988 and is now a senior examiner. In this series he has also written the Notes on *The Merchant of Venice*.

The text used in these Notes is the Longman New Swan Shakespeare, edited by H.M. Hulme (Longman, 1995).

Health Warning: This study guide will enhance your understanding, but should not replace the reading of the original text and/or study in class.

PART ONE

INTRODUCTION

HOW TO STUDY A PLAY

You have bought this book because you wanted to study a play on your own. This may supplement classwork.

- Drama is a special 'kind' of writing (the technical term is 'genre') because it needs a performance in the theatre to arrive at a full interpretation of its meaning. When reading a play you have to imagine how it should be performed; the words alone will not be sufficient. Think of gestures and movements.

- Drama is always about conflict of some sort (it may be below the surface). Identify the conflicts in the play and you will be close to identifying the large ideas or themes which bind all the parts together.

- Make careful notes on themes, characters, plot and any sub-plots of the play.

- Playwrights find non-realistic ways of allowing an audience to see into the minds and motives of their characters. The 'soliloquy', in which a character speaks directly to the audience, is one such device. Does the play you are studying have any such passages?

- Which characters do you like or dislike in the play? Why? Do your sympathies change as you see more of these characters?

- Think of the playwright writing the play. Why were these particular arrangements of events, these particular sets of characters and these particular speeches chosen?

Studying on your own requires self-discipline and a carefully thought-out work plan in order to be effective. Good luck.

His family   William Shakespeare (1564–1616) was born in Stratford-on-Avon and baptised there in Holy Trinity Church on 26 April 1564. His family was quite wealthy, his father was a successful merchant and held several important offices in the town. William was educated at the grammar school in Stratford, where he would have learnt the common school subjects of the day: Latin, history, rhetoric (see Literary Terms) and logic (reasoning).

His marriage   He married Anne Hathaway of neighbouring Shottery in 1582, when she was already pregnant with his child. William was eighteen when they married, Anne was twenty-six. They had a daughter, Susanna, in May 1583, and twins, Hamnet and Judith, in 1585. It is thought that Shakespeare left Stratford around 1585, having possibly spent some time as a schoolmaster.

At work in London   He is next heard of in London, where he met the Earl of Southampton, the man who was to become his patron. He is mentioned in records of 1592 as being an actor and dramatist in London. He is listed as an actor in the original performances of Ben Jonson's *Every Man in his Humour* in 1598 and *Sejanus* in 1603. After this he probably concentrated on his own work.

The Globe Theatre   By 1599 he was important enough to be involved in the establishment of a new theatre, the Globe, on the south bank of the Thames. He wrote many plays for the Globe, and performed in them with his company, the King's Players. (In 1995 an authentic reconstruction of the Globe Theatre opened close to the original site.) *Julius Caesar* is thought to have been written around 1599 and was first published in 1623, although it had been performed frequently before this.

Return to Stratford   In 1597 Shakespeare bought New Place, a large house in Stratford, and much land around the town. He retired to New Place in 1611, though he still visited

London and maintained links with actors and theatre life. He died in Stratford on 23 April 1616 and was buried in Holy Trinity Church.

A sixteenth-century success story

William Shakespeare was a very successful and famous man in his own day. He was a favourite playwright of Queen Elizabeth and of her successor, James I. His careful cultivation of royal approval and his links with the Earl of Southampton gave him a privileged position. Shakespeare's plays were well liked by the public and he became very wealthy. It is difficult to think of a modern equivalent, but famous film-makers such as Stephen Spielberg and Orson Welles are probably the closest comparisons. By today's standards, Shakespeare was a self-made millionaire, a difficult achievement in the twentieth century and a quite remarkable one in the sixteenth.

CONTEXT & SETTING

THE HISTORICAL PERSPECTIVE

Gaius Julius Caesar (100–44BC)

The men of patrician families had ruled Rome before the Republic was founded in 510BC.

Caesar was born of a patrician (noble) family, ensuring him wealth and status. He forged a career as a soldier and statesman and, in 60BC, with two other patricians, Pompey and Crassus, formed the first Triumvirate. The three men shared power in Rome. Caesar deliberately sought to please the plebians (the ordinary people) and thus made enemies among the older aristocratic families.

He married three times: Cinna's daughter Cornelia in 84BC, Pompeia in 68BC (divorced in 62BC) and Calpurnia in 59BC.

Caesar's power and popularity increased as a result of his successful military campaigns. He conquered Gaul (approximately modern France) between 58BC and 50BC and landed in Britain in 55BC. The loyalty of his armies was directly to him rather than to the government, so making him more enemies among the old noble families, who feared his increasing power.

The death of Crassus in 53BC ended the Triumvirate and for the next few years Pompey allied himself with the Senate (the ruling council), while Caesar maintained control of a large army. Good relations between Pompey and Caesar had, until this time, been maintained by the fact that Pompey was married to Caesar's daughter, Julia.

'To cross the Rubicon' has become a figure of speech (see Literary Terms) meaning to take a drastic and irreversible step.

The Senate was concerned by the popularity and military independence of Caesar and in 50BC asked Caesar to relinquish command of his armies. He refused, and in 49BC led his legions across the River Rubicon (then the northern frontier of Italy), thus initiating civil war.

Pompey fought against Caesar but was defeated by him at Pharsalus, in Greece, in 48BC. Pompey fled to Egypt but was later murdered by the Egyptians. Caesar spent the following winter in Alexandria with Cleopatra, by whom he is said to have had a son, Caesarion. He defeated the remnants of Pompey's supporters in the battles of Thapsus (46BC) and Munda (45BC) and then returned to Rome, finding it in a state of civil unrest.

Two Consuls, powerful magistrates, held supreme civil and military power in Rome.

Caesar was elected Consul and the Senate made him Dictator in order to suppress the riots. Mark Antony was made commander of the cavalry.

Caesar introduced sweeping reforms to the government of Rome. He increased the number of senators to nine hundred by bringing in new members from the provinces and the army. This meant that the senators from the old families were outnumbered. He also assumed the power to declare war; previously only the Senate could do this.

The Tarquin dynasty ruled Rome from 753 BC to 510 BC.

These reforms angered the old families of Rome who saw their long-held power being eroded. Caesar even minted coins bearing his head and appointed his own officials. He then demanded the right to call himself King, when away from Rome, in order to impress his enemies. Kings had been hated in Rome since the days of the Tarquins.

Some of the senators feared Caesar's ambition, thinking that he was going to proclaim himself Emperor. They favoured a republican government, with the Senate holding power. Caesar was assassinated on the steps of the Senate on the Ides of March (15 March) 44 BC by a group of Republicans including Brutus and Cassius, on the very day that he was to accept the crown.

The play in context

An Elizabethan playgoer would have been quite familiar with some of the stories of Ancient Greece and Ancient Rome. Shakespeare based many of his plays on stories in well-known sources such as Holinshead's *Chronicles* and, in the case of *Julius Caesar*, Plutarch's *Lives of the Greeks and Romans* (written in the first century AD). In it Plutarch describes the assassination of Caesar:

> Men report that Caesar did still defend himself against the rest, running every way with his body. But when he saw Brutus with his sword drawn in his hand, then he pulled his gown over his head and made no more resistance.

Here, as in his other plays, Shakespeare shaped the work of other authors to his own dramatic ends.

The Elizabethan world was a very different one from our own. People held beliefs that we would now consider strange. One of the most important of these was that the earthly world was linked closely to the

world of God and that what happened on earth had
consequences in Heaven. If an important person such as
a king were to be killed unjustly, then Heaven would be
disturbed and this would in turn result in unnatural
events on earth. The terrible storm in Act I, Scene 3 is
symbolic of unrest in Heaven.

PART TWO

SUMMARIES

GENERAL SUMMARY

Act I　　　The play opens on 15 February 44BC, the feast of
Lupercalia. This spring festival is now being used as a
holiday in honour of Julius Caesar. The ordinary
citizens are celebrating his triumphs, but not everyone
is delighted by his success. Two tribunes, Murellus and
Flavius, are incensed by the fickleness of the people.
They say that the citizens have quickly forgotten 'great
Pompey', recently killed by Caesar, and now celebrate
Caesar's every act.

Caesar's triumphal procession enters and a soothsayer
warns Caesar to 'beware the Ides of March'. Cassius
sounds out Brutus in order to find what his opinion of
Caesar really is. Cassius is resentful of Caesar's
popularity and feels that Caesar is no better than many
other noble Romans. The men hear a shout from the
crowd offstage. This surprises Brutus and causes him to
admit that he too is unhappy at the idea that the people
might choose to make Caesar king. Cassius tells Brutus
that Caesar is not really a great man but has weaknesses
like anyone else. Cassius condemns Caesar and reveals
his jealousy of him.

Casca now gives an amusing account of the manner in
which Caesar manipulated the crowd at the games and
refused the crown three times, even though he clearly
wanted to take it. Cassius is left on his own and reveals
to the audience that he is planning to deceive Brutus
into joining a plot against Caesar.

A terrifying storm breaks over Rome. People report
unnatural events, such as tame lions walking the streets.
Casca feels that the storm is a warning from the gods

that something bad is about to happen. Cassius, on the other hand, walks calmly through the streets and welcomes the storm as a parallel to the actions of Caesar. When Cassius tests the feelings Casca has for Caesar it becomes clear that the assassination plot is already well developed.

Act II It is now the Ides of March (15 March). Brutus has had some time to consider joining the conspiracy against Caesar. He is deeply troubled by the conflict between his feelings for Caesar and his fears about what he is doing to Rome. The conspirators visit Brutus at his house and he welcomes them. Cassius wants to kill Caesar and his principal supporters, such as Mark Antony. Brutus persuades the conspirators that the plot should involve only Caesar. This is agreed.

Portia shows her devotion to her husband and reveals her courage. She has wounded herself in the thigh and never complained of the pain. This convinces Brutus that he can tell her of the plot to kill Caesar.

Calpurnia tells Caesar of a terrifying dream she had that night. Caesar tells Decius of her dream, in which Caesar's statue ran with blood, and says that he will stay at home. Decius is desperate to take Caesar to the Senate and so interprets the dream as a good omen. Caesar believes him and is also afraid of being laughed at and so decides to go to the Capitol (the hill in Rome on which stood the Temple of Jupiter). The conspirators arrive to escort him.

Artemidorus has prepared a written warning for Caesar. Portia is anxious for her husband as she knows the serious consequences of what he is about to do.

Act III

Caesar approaches the Capitol. He is accompanied by the conspirators. Artemidorus tries to give his petition to Caesar but Caesar rejects it. The conspirators surround Caesar, pretending to ask for clemency for the brother of Metellus, one of the conspirators. Caesar is struck from behind and the conspirators stab him. The final wound is inflicted by Brutus. Caesar's killers bathe their hands in his blood.

Antony arrives and sees the body of Caesar. He tells the conspirators that if they are going to kill him they should do so now. Brutus tells him that they mean him no harm and offers him his friendship. Antony then shakes the bloody hand of each of the conspirators, addressing each one by name. Brutus promises to give Antony good reasons why Caesar had to be killed. Antony asks to be allowed to give the **oration** (see Literary Terms) at Caesar's funeral. Cassius does not want this but is overruled by Brutus. Antony is permitted to speak immediately after Brutus.

Antony is left alone on stage and speaks his true mind. He is clearly still loyal to Caesar and will seek revenge for his murder. No sooner has Antony prophesied civil war than a messenger arrives saying that Octavius, Caesar's great-nephew and heir, is coming to Rome. Antony plans to test the loyalty of the citizens of Rome in his speech at the funeral.

Brutus addresses the crowd, giving them a reasoned argument as to why Caesar had to die. Brutus is a good public speaker and the crowd is impressed by what he has to say. Mark Antony then speaks but his oration is addressed to the hearts of the people. He constantly refers to the conspirators as 'honourable men'. Antony also reads Caesar's generous will to the crowd. When he has finished his emotional appeal the citizens have decided that Brutus and the rest were traitors, not 'honourable men'. The crowd takes to the streets, looking for anyone connected with Caesar's death. In their blind fury they kill Cinna the poet who is not a conspirator, but has the same name as one of the conspirators.

Act IV   Antony, Octavius and Lepidus are in control in Rome. Brutus and Cassius, who have fled to Sardis in Asia Minor (modern Turkey), are becoming hostile to one another. Portia is dead. The Roman army under Antony and Octavius is marching on Philippi in north-eastern Greece. Brutus overrules Cassius once again and the two rebels agree to lead their armies to Philippi to fight Antony and Octavius there. The ghost of Caesar appears to Brutus and says that he will see him again at Philippi.

Act V   The generals meet on the battlefield before the fighting begins. Once battle commences, Brutus is successful against Octavius whereas Cassius is defeated by Antony. Cassius orders his servant Pindarus to kill him. Brutus is then defeated and runs upon his own sword, killing himself. Mark Antony says that Brutus was 'the noblest Roman of them all'.

DETAILED SUMMARIES

ACT I

SCENE 1

A public area of Rome   Two tribunes, Flavius and Murellus, enter to find that a crowd has gathered. Flavius orders the crowd to disperse, saying that today is not a holiday. They are teased by a cobbler who gets the better of them by making puns (see Literary Terms). The cobbler says that people have gathered to rejoice in Caesar's triumph.

Pompey had been This infuriates Flavius and Murellus who say that the
defeated by Caesar same crowd that has now gathered to welcome home
four years earlier. the victorious Caesar, once greeted 'great Pompey'.
Murellus points out that Caesar has not brought any
riches to Rome recently and so should not be treated as
if he were a great victor returning with the spoils of
war. Murellus is also incensed that Caesar should be
worshipped when he was responsible for the fall of
Pompey.

Flavius and Murellus leave, vowing to remove any
A great Roman decorations from images of Caesar. It is the feast of
festival celebrating Lupercalia and so many statues are 'decked with
the earth's fertility. ceremonies' (scarves and ribbons). Flavius feels that
Caesar has grown too important for his own good.

COMMENT Caesar maintained his popularity by holding lavish
public festivals. Here he has arranged a great
celebration on the day of Lupercalia.

Shakespeare has reduced the time between events.
Lupercalia was actually held on 15 February; here it is
the day before the Ides of March (15 March).

GLOSSARY
tribune a magistrate from a plebeian (ordinary) family, elected
to defend the interests of the plebeians against the power of
the patricians
being mechanical working with one's hands
cobbler both a shoemaker and a poor workman
naughty good for nothing; a forceful insult
awl a tool for making holes in leather; here the pun is with 'all'
tributaries captured enemies who were forced to pay tribute
money
Pompey's blood the sons of Pompey whom Caesar has recently
defeated in battle
intermit delay or prevent
basest lowest
metal a pun on mettle, meaning character

SCENE 2

A street in Rome

Caesar, Calpurnia, Antony, Brutus and others are making their way to the races held to celebrate the feast of Lupercalia. Antony is to take part in the races and Caesar asks him to touch Calpurnia as he runs, in order to make her fertile (able to have children).

A soothsayer calls to Caesar from the crowd and Caesar turns to hear what he has to say. The soothsayer utters the famous line, 'Beware the Ides of March'. Caesar dismisses him as a dreamer and moves on.

Brutus loves Caesar but does not want him to become king.

Cassius and Brutus are left on stage and Cassius says that he has noticed how unhappy Brutus has looked recently. The cheers of the crowd at the games can be heard and Brutus lets slip that he is worried the people may be about to choose Caesar as king. Cassius is intrigued to hear that Brutus does not want Caesar to be king and tells him that he is also unhappy at Caesar's growing power.

Soon the emperor would be regarded as both a king and a god.

Cassius tells Brutus of two occasions on which Caesar appeared to be very weak. Caesar had challenged Cassius to swim the River Tiber, which flows through Rome, with him. Cassius swam it easily but Caesar nearly drowned and had to be rescued. Cassius carried Caesar from the water. Later, when in Spain, Caesar developed a fever and cried 'as a sick girl' for water.

Cassius has seen Caesar at his weakest and cannot accept that he is supposed to treat him as a god.

Cassius clearly hates Caesar.

Cassius goes on to say that Rome has not had one ruler for many years and that no single man should rule Rome. Brutus will not commit himself to this extent, but does say that he would rather be a villager than live in Rome under Caesar.

Caesar and his party enter. Caesar looks annoyed and immediately comments to Antony that he does not like the 'lean and hungry look' he sees on the face of Cassius. Caesar does not trust him and says that, if he feared anyone, it would be Cassius.

Brutus stops Casca, one of the group that has been at the games, in order to find out what had taken place to cause the crowd to cheer so. Casca says that the crowd cheered as Antony offered the crown to Caesar. It was offered three times and each time Caesar refused it. It appeared to Casca that this had been deliberately staged and that Caesar was actually very reluctant not to take the crown. Caesar then fainted in the market-place after saying he would cut his own throat if the people of Rome asked him.

Signs of opposition to Caesar are suppressed.

Cicero commented on the events, but spoke in Greek so that few could understand him. Murellus and Flavius have been 'put to silence' for pulling scarves from statues of Caesar. Cassius, Casca and Brutus arrange to meet the following day. Cassius is not sure of Brutus's support. He decides to throw some messages, supposedly written by Roman citizens, through the window of Brutus's house, in the hope of swaying his opinion. The messages will praise Brutus and hint at Caesar's ambition.

COMMENT

Note the way that Calpurnia and Antony address Caesar at the start of this scene. They treat him as their lord.

It is ironic (see Literary Terms) that the first words
Brutus speaks in the play are to warn Caesar of the Ides
of March: Brutus is to become a leading figure in the
plot to assassinate Caesar on this very date.

Romans worshipped their ancestors. The greater the
ancestor, the more noble a Roman could claim to be.

Caesar refers to himself in the third person, i.e. 'Caesar'
rather than 'I'.

Many important Romans wanted Rome to remain a
republic. They strongly opposed the idea of there being
a king again.

GLOSSARY

press crowd

soothsayer a fortune-teller

a common laughter a fool who tries to amuse everyone

as lief rather

bear the palm carry the symbol of victory

Colossus the Colossus of Rhodes was one of the seven wonders
of the ancient world; it was a huge statue, said to have stood
with one foot on each side of the entrance to the harbour at
Rhodes

meet correct, appropriate

Cicero (106–43BC) a famous speaker

swoond fainted

the falling sickness probably epilepsy

SCENE 3

*A street in
Rome on a
stormy night*

*The natural order
of the world seems
disturbed.*

Casca meets Cicero and describes various strange
phenomena. He thinks they are omens that something
terrible is to occur. The things he has seen are:
fire dropping from the sky; a slave who held up his
hand which burst into flames, yet he was not burnt; a
lion which passed him in the street but did not seem to
see him; men on fire walking the streets; a bird of night
(probably an owl) at mid-day.

Cassius enters as Cicero leaves. He has been walking
about in the terrible storm, tempting fate by not

sheltering from the lightning. He says that the strange events which have taken place are the result of heaven's impatience. He likens the storms which have turned Nature upside down to Caesar's actions. Cassius tells Casca that Caesar, with his lust for power, is to blame for the upset in Nature.

Casca reveals that Caesar is to be crowned king by the senators on the following day. Cassius says that he would rather commit suicide using his own dagger, than live in Rome under Caesar. Cassius has arranged to meet several important Romans at Pompey's monument. They are to discuss a matter of great importance and 'dangerous consequence'.

The messages will appear to have come from ordinary Romans.

Cinna arrives, on his way to meet Cassius. He asks Cassius to attempt to enlist Brutus's support. Cassius has already thought of a way of persuading Brutus to help in the conspiracy to murder Caesar. He asks Cinna to place forged messages where Brutus will find them and to throw one in at his window. Casca comments that the presence of Brutus would change the people's opinion of the conspirators as Brutus is loved throughout Rome. Cassius is sure that he can persuade Brutus to join them.

COMMENT The many unnatural events described by Casca help to increase tension and would have emphasised to an Elizabethan audience that momentous events would occur.

Romans considered it honourable to commit suicide.

Cassius is quite prepared to lie to Brutus in order to enlist his help.

Many Romans feel they are behaving properly in ridding Rome of Caesar and thus preserving the Republic.

It is fitting that the conspirators should meet at
Pompey's monument as Caesar defeated Pompey in
battle to achieve power in Rome.

GLOSSARY   rived split
                not sensible of not feeling the effect of
                ghastly women women who looked like ghosts
                prodigies extraordinary and awful signs
                conjointly occur together
                want lack, be without
                thews muscles
                bondman slave
                fleering flattering
                Pompey's porch a monument to Pompey who was defeated by
                  Caesar
                alchemy the art of turning base metals into gold; it led to
                  discoveries in chemistry

A Identify the speaker.

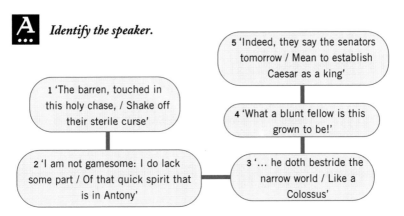

5 'Indeed, they say the senators tomorrow / Mean to establish Caesar as a king'

1 'The barren, touched in this holy chase, / Shake off their sterile curse'

4 'What a blunt fellow is this grown to be!'

2 'I am not gamesome: I do lack some part / Of that quick spirit that is in Antony'

3 '... he doth bestride the narrow world / Like a Colossus'

Identify the person 'to whom' this comment refers.

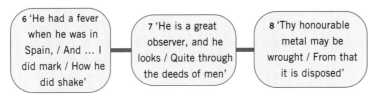

6 'He had a fever when he was in Spain, / And ... I did mark / How he did shake'

7 'He is a great observer, and he looks / Quite through the deeds of men'

8 'Thy honourable metal may be wrought / From that it is disposed'

Check your answers on page 69.

B Consider these issues.

a Why Shakespeare has chosen not to portray Cassius as a sympathetic character. (Remember Cassius is the driving force behind the initial plot to kill Caesar.)

b How far the unnatural events described in Scene 3 are due to Caesar's imminent coronation and how much they are due to his murder.

c Brutus has to be tricked into joining the plot but there may be signs that he has become unhappy with Caesar's behaviour.

d Brutus lets slip the fact that he fears Caesar will be made king. How far does this give Cassius power over him?

e To what extent the audience is allowed to see the human side of Caesar.

f How cleverly Cassius exploits the fears of many Romans about life under a king.

ACT II

SCENE 1

Brutus's villa at night

Brutus delivers a long **soliloquy** (see Literary Terms) in which he debates the rights and wrongs of killing Caesar. Brutus says that he has no personal reason for wishing Caesar dead but that he fears what Caesar would become if he were crowned. Brutus compares Caesar's progress to an ambitious man climbing a ladder, saying that once he has reached the top he might turn his back on the ladder and look down upon everyone. He decides that Caesar must be killed now, before he attains complete power, just as it is easier to kill a serpent when it is in the egg than when it has hatched.

This lets the audience know the assassination is near.

Lucius brings Brutus a paper which he has found by the window. Brutus asks if the Ides of March is tomorrow and then reads the letter. It tells him to 'awake' and to 'speak, strike' and 'redress'. He recalls that his ancestors drove the evil King Tarquin from Rome and decides that he must act in the same way. Lucius returns and tells his master 'fourteen days are wasted (passed)' so that it is 15 March. Brutus has been troubled since Cassius first spoke to him against Caesar.

Lucius announces the arrival of Cassius and a group of men in disguise. Brutus remarks that not even Erebus

Cassius fears that Mark Antony might seek revenge for Caesar's death. (Hell) would be dark enough to hide the men who killed Caesar. Cassius wants the conspirators to swear an oath, but Brutus refuses, saying that that is the action of lesser men who need to give themselves reasons for action. Metellus says that he thinks the great orator, Cicero, should be involved but Brutus points out that Cicero would not be involved in something that he had not himself started.

Cassius suggests that Mark Antony should be assassinated along with Caesar. Brutus is against this as he feels it would make the conspirators appear to be 'too bloody' and more like butchers than sacrificers. Cassius comments on Caesar's growing superstition and worries that he may take the events of the night as a warning and so not venture forth. Decius says that he will play on Caesar's superstitious nature and bring him to the Capitol. The conspirators leave Brutus alone and his wife, Portia, enters. She asks him why he has been so troubled lately and he replies that he has not been well. Portia says that he should, therefore, be in bed. She knows that he has met several people in secret and thinks his sickness is of the mind rather than the body. In order to prove her courage and her ability to keep a secret, she recently wounded herself in the thigh yet never complained of the pain. Brutus says he is not worthy of her and promises to tell her everything. They are interrupted by a knock at the door. It is Caius Ligarius, come to join the conspiracy. Brutus leaves with him.

COMMENT   Note the frequent use of the image of a snake or serpent throughout Brutus's soliloquy. The serpent has particular significance because of the story of Adam and Eve.

Brutus does not respond quickly to the idea of killing Caesar.

Brutus makes a mistake in underestimating Mark Antony, believing he would be powerless without Caesar.

Brutus keeps the secret of the plot from his wife. She is hurt by this.

GLOSSARY   spurn at kick

common proof a matter of common experience

exhalations here the word refers to meteors which have been 'exhaled' from the heavens

Shall Rome etc. it is clear that Brutus has read this sort of thing before

palter cheat

cautelous deceiving

purgers surgeons; they drew off what they believed to be bad blood in order to purge the body of infection

augurers priests who interpreted omens

rheumy and unpurged air air that has not been 'purged' by the sun

to wear a kerchief to be ill

SCENE 2

Caesar's house in the early morning of 15 March

Caesar has been disturbed by the storm and his wife has talked of murder in her sleep. He orders the priests to make sacrifices and to bring him news of the results.

Calpurnia asks Caesar not to leave the house but he says that he refuses to show fear. She tells him what she has heard of the night's strange events and feels that they can only indicate the death of someone great. News arrives from the priests; they have cut open a beast which had no heart – a very bad omen.

Caesar agrees to allow Mark Antony to go to the Senate and say that he is not well. Decius Brutus arrives and is told by Caesar that he will not be going to the Senate house. Decius asks for a reason and tells Caesar that the senators will laugh at him otherwise. Caesar tells Decius of Calpurnia's dream, in which his statue

Decius knows that vanity is Caesar's weaknesses.

ran with blood and Romans came to bathe their hands in it. Decius interprets the dream favourably, saying that it signifies Rome sucking 'Reviving blood' from Caesar.

Caesar allows his pride to rule his head.

Decius goes on to say that the Senate intend to crown Caesar today but that the senators might change their minds if Caesar does not appear and mock him for living by his wife's dreams. Caesar is taken in by the words of Decius and resolves to go. Brutus and several of the conspirators enter, followed by Mark Antony. Caesar asks Trebonius to stay close to him and Trebonius remarks, in an **aside** (see Literary Terms), that he will be so close that Caesar's friends might wish he had been further away.

Brutus is troubled that he is merely acting like a friend and not actually being a friend to Caesar.

COMMENT

Priests sacrificed animals, cut them open and believed they could make predictions by examining the state of the dead animal's organs.

Caesar takes pains to point out that he chooses not to go to the Senate as opposed to being unable to go.

With **dramatic irony** (see Literary Terms), Caesar asks Trebonius to keep near to him.

Brutus is troubled by his conscience, he is still unsure that he is taking the right course.

GLOSSARY

whelped given birth
hurtled clashed
purposed decided, preordained
greybeards old men
ague illness
earns grieves

SCENE 3

A street near the Capitol

Artemidorus is reading aloud a message that he has written. It is a warning to Caesar and gives the names of the conspirators, saying that they have no love for Caesar. Artemidorus decides to wait for Caesar to pass and then give him the message in the hope of saving his life.

COMMENT

The message written by Artemidorus could save Caesar's life if he takes the time to read it.

SCENE 4

Outside Brutus's house

Portia tries to send Lucius on an errand to the Capitol to observe Brutus. She says she is worried about her husband's health and asks to be kept informed of anyone who approaches Caesar. A soothsayer enters and Portia questions him about his business. He tells her that he is waiting for Caesar as he fears for his safety. Portia finally sends Lucius to speak to Brutus, to say she is merry and to come back and tell her of his response.

COMMENT

This short scene, together with the previous one, establishes that Caesar may well be warned about the intended assassination, thus increasing the dramatic tension.

GLOSSARY   praetors important judges

Identify the speaker.

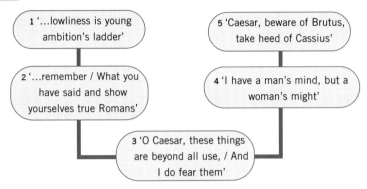

1 '...lowliness is young ambition's ladder'

5 'Caesar, beware of Brutus, take heed of Cassius'

2 '...remember / What you have said and show yourselves true Romans'

4 'I have a man's mind, but a woman's might'

3 'O Caesar, these things are beyond all use, / And I do fear them'

Identify the person 'to whom' this comment refers.

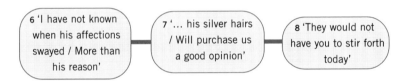

6 'I have not known when his affections swayed / More than his reason'

7 '... his silver hairs / Will purchase us a good opinion'

8 'They would not have you to stir forth today'

Check your answers on page 69.

 Consider these issues.

a To what extent Brutus is torn between his personal feelings for Caesar and what he thinks are his own responsibilities to Rome.

b How far the lies told by Cassius are responsible for swaying Brutus in his decision.

c How Shakespeare develops the relationship between Portia and Brutus and how this becomes important later in the play.

d The part that Caesar's vanity plays in sending him to the Capitol against the wishes of his wife.

e The differences between the relationships of the two couples: Caesar and Calpurnia and Brutus and Portia.

f The ways in which religious superstition can be seen to influence characters in the play.

ACT III

SCENE 1

A street close to the Capitol

Fate is clearly working against Caesar here.

Caesar enters with Brutus and the conspirators, Antony, Artemidorus, the soothsayer and other Romans. Artemidorus gives Caesar his petition but Caesar does not read it because Decius gives him another. Artemidorus protests, saying that his is the more important as it affects Caesar directly, but Caesar says this is the very reason for reading it last.

The group enters the Capitol and Popillius, who seems to have found out about the plot, joins Caesar. This worries Cassius as he fears the conspirators are about to be caught, but Brutus assures him they are safe. Trebonius draws Antony away while Metellus approaches Caesar with a petition. Metellus wants his brother's banishment repealed but Caesar tells him not to beg. Brutus joins the appeal, kneeling at Caesar's feet, yet Caesar remains firm. He compares himself to the sun, the one constant star which does not move in the heavens.

Metellus's appeal is the signal to attack.

Caesar is attacked and stabbed many times. As Brutus attacks him he utters his last words then dies. Cinna and Cassius want to shout the news of their deed in the streets but Brutus prevents them from glorifying their actions.

Trebonius announces that Antony has fled. Brutus tells the conspirators to bathe their arms in Caesar's blood and show Rome that it is now free from tyranny. A servant arrives from Antony, bringing an offer of peace. Antony has asked that Brutus tell him why Caesar had to die and promises to follow Brutus if the answer is convincing. Cassius is worried about Antony.

An assassination such as this often led to mass retaliations against the dead man's followers.

Antony enters and confronts Caesar's murderers. He says that if they intend to kill him then there is no better time than the present and no better weapons than those which killed Caesar. Brutus assures Antony that he will not be harmed and that he will explain his actions once the people of Rome have been told there is nothing for them to fear.

Note that Antony calls Caesar 'Julius'; a sign of friendship.

Antony makes a point of shaking the bloody hand of each of the murderers. He praises Caesar and asks for his forgiveness for now befriending his killers. Cassius asks if Antony intends to be a friend to the conspirators. Antony says that he will be a friend to them if they can give him reasons why it was necessary for Caesar to die. Antony then asks for permission to take the body of Caesar to the market-place and to speak at his funeral. Cassius is troubled by this as he fears what Antony might say, but Brutus decides to speak first and so assure the crowd of the need for Caesar's death. Brutus tells Antony not to blame the conspirators in his speech but to speak well of Caesar.

Antony is left alone with the body of Caesar. He says that Caesar was the noblest man ever to have lived and prophesies doom for those who killed him. Antony *This is the sign for* foresees bloody civil war and acts of great horror. He *mass plunder and* says that Caesar's spirit will 'cry havoc' and that many *slaughter.* dead men will need burying.

A servant of Octavius enters and tells Antony that his master is approaching the city. Antony says that Octavius should wait outside the city until he has made his funeral **oration** (see Literary Terms) and tested the loyalty of the people of Rome.

COMMENT   Caesar's first words in this scene have great impact because of the earlier conversation between Brutus and his servant.

Caesar speaks of himself in the third person 'Caesar'. This could be seen as a touch of arrogance on his part.

By presenting his petition, Metellus allows the conspirators to surround Caesar.

The words 'Et tu, Brute?' are very famous. They reveal Caesar's surprise that even Brutus has attacked him.

Caesar is killed at the foot of Pompey's statue. This is very **ironic** (see Literary Terms) as Caesar himself defeated Pompey in battle to take power in Rome.

Antony makes sure he knows who the conspirators are and makes a mental note of each man's name. Cassius has good reason to be worried about Antony. In this speech Antony calls some of the conspirators by two names. Romans generally had three names: the *praenomen*, like our Christian or first name; the *nomen*, the name of the clan; the *cognomen* which was the name of the family. It was rare for someone to use all three of their names, and as the plays shows, most people were called by a single name. Antony's use of two names when speaking to some of the conspirators helps underline the tenseness of the occasion.

Antony's true intentions are revealed in lines 254–279. He speaks powerfully and the audience knows from this speech that his funeral oration (see Literary Terms) will rouse the people of Rome.

Only a king could 'cry havoc', give the order for destruction.

GLOSSARY

sirrah fellow

puissant powerful

fond foolish

base spaniel fawning low cringing like a dog

enfranchisement the right to vote

firmament heavens

Olympus a Greek mountain, said to be the home of the gods

bootless without success

'Et tu, Brute?' 'Even you, Brutus?'

Pompey's basis the foot of Pompey's statue

reek steam

cumber burden, weigh down

Até the Greek goddess of revenge

SCENE *2*

The market-place in Rome

Brutus and Cassius enter with the ordinary people of the city. The two men arrange to speak separately to the people. Brutus addresses the crowd and tells them that he killed Caesar because he loved Rome even more than he loved Caesar. He asks them if they would rather be slaves and Caesar alive or freemen and Caesar dead. Brutus adds that he killed Caesar because of Caesar's ambition. When he asks the crowd whether anyone wishes to cease being a Roman in Rome as it is now, no one comes forward. Antony brings in the body of Caesar as Brutus offers the people of Rome his own life should they wish it. The people acclaim Brutus as he leaves Antony to speak.

Brutus is recognised as a great public figure.

Antony begins his address to a hostile crowd who are very much in favour of Brutus. The plebeians say that they are glad to be rid of Caesar and that Antony had better not say anything against Brutus.

He begins his speech by asking for their attention and
says that he has not come to praise Caesar. Antony
comments that a man's goodness dies with him but that
his evil deeds live on after him. He refers to the
statement that Brutus made about Caesar's ambition.
Antony says that Caesar has paid for this ambition. He
then refers to Brutus and the conspirators as honourable
men, before repeating again that Brutus said Caesar was
ambitious. Antony then gives examples of some of
Caesar's actions:

• He brought many captives back to Rome whose
  ransoms filled the city's coffers
• When the poor cried, Caesar wept with them
• Caesar refused the crown three times

Antony
deliberately makes
Brutus appear
dishonourable.

These statements are punctuated by the comment that
Brutus says Caesar was ambitious. Antony reminds the
crowd that each person there loved Caesar at one time
and so should now mourn his death.

This speech is well received by the crowd. Antony tells
the people to remain loyal to the conspirators, who are,
after all, honourable men. He then produces Caesar's
will but says he dare not read it as it would prove how
much Caesar loved the people of Rome. The crowd
shouts for the will to be read. Antony refuses, saying
that the will would only inflame the people; they insist
that he reads it. Antony descends to the body of Caesar
and asks the crowd to join him. By now the crowd has
turned against Brutus and the conspirators whom they
call traitors.

Antony lifts Caesar's cloak, torn by the conspirators'
daggers, and shows it to the crowd. He says that the
'unkindest cut of all' was made by Brutus whom Caesar
loved. Antony describes the murder of Caesar and,
finally, shows the people the body of Caesar. The
people become enraged and swear vengeance upon the

Antony has already stirred the crowd with his speech.

conspirators. Antony says that if he were a great orator such as Brutus, he would stir the people to avenge Caesar's death. Finally, he reads Caesar's will. Besides seventy-five drachmas for each citizen, Caesar has bequeathed his private gardens and orchards to the people. The crowd is now incensed and leaves with Caesar's body, saying that Caesar's funeral fire will be used to light torches to burn the houses of the traitors.

Octavius has arrived in Rome and Antony leaves to meet him at Caesar's house. Brutus and Cassius have fled the city.

COMMENT Brutus's speech is accepted by the crowd and, when he has finished speaking, the people are very much on his side.

The speech of Antony mirrors that given by Brutus.

Antony cleverly sways the opinion of the crowd without attacking the conspirators directly.

In his **oration** (see Literary Terms), Antony keeps repeating that Brutus is an honourable man, but follows this with statements intended to suggest the opposite.

After Antony's first speech the people begin to side with him. His speech by Caesar's body and the reading of his will are carefully calculated to turn the people against the conspirators.

The speech of Brutus is in **prose** (see Literary Terms) whereas Antony addresses the crowd in powerful **blank verse** (see Literary Terms).

GLOSSARY interred buried
general coffers public funds
commons ordinary citizens
issue children

the Nervii a fierce Gallic tribe whom Caesar defeated in a great
  battle

drachmas silver coins

walks gardens

SCENE 3

A street

Cinna, the poet, is confronted by a mob of angry citizens. They ask him many questions and when he tells them his name they kill him, because Cinna is the name of one of the conspirators.

COMMENT

This scene illustrates the fury of the mob. It also serves as a warning about the nature of vengeance and mob rule.

GLOSSARY

fantasy imagination

bear me a bang take a blow from me

Identify the speaker.

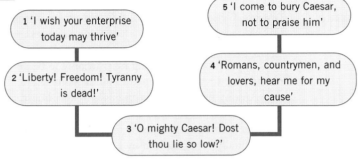

1 'I wish your enterprise today may thrive'

5 'I come to bury Caesar, not to praise him'

2 'Liberty! Freedom! Tyranny is dead!'

4 'Romans, countrymen, and lovers, hear me for my cause'

3 'O mighty Caesar! Dost thou lie so low?'

Identify the person 'to whom' this comment refers.

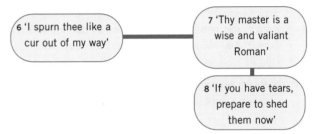

6 'I spurn thee like a cur out of my way'

7 'Thy master is a wise and valiant Roman'

8 'If you have tears, prepare to shed them now'

Check your answers on page 69.

 B **Consider these issues.**

a Caesar is stubborn about the banishment of Metellus's brother. How far does this confirm the view of the conspirators?

b Caesar dies immediately after his friend, Brutus, had stabbed him. Why might it be important that it is Brutus who strikes the final blow?

c Some productions of the play have Caesar dropping his guard to allow Brutus to stab him. Think about the different interpretations of Caesar's death that are possible.

d Why the conspirators do not feel they are making a mistake in not killing Antony.

e Why Brutus allows Antony to address the people of Rome at all.

f Whether or not Brutus is really a good judge of character.

ACT IV

SCENE 1

A nobleman's house

Antony, Octavius and Lepidus discuss which of the traitors must die. The list they draw up includes members of their own families. Once Lepidus leaves, Antony criticises him, saying he is fit only to be an errand boy. Octavius defends Lepidus, pointing out that Antony treated him as an equal in deciding that Lepidus's brother should be on the list of those who must die. Antony responds by likening Lepidus to his horse, finally insulting him by saying that Lepidus is always behind the times with his ideas.

Antony says that Brutus and Cassius are raising an army and Octavius replies that they must prepare their own forces too. Octavius is worried that he and Antony have many secret enemies as well as those who are openly against them.

COMMENT

Antony proves himself to be a shrewd judge of men, though a harsh one.

GLOSSARY

prick'd marked off with a pin-prick on the list
unmeritable unworthy
levying powers raising armies
sit in council decide

SCENE 2

The camp of Brutus at Sardis

Brutus is unhappy with the actions of Cassius and some of his officers. Lucilius says that although Cassius received him with 'courtesy and respect enough', it was not with the warmth of earlier times. Cassius enters and accuses Brutus of having wronged him. Brutus tells Cassius not to speak like that in front of the soldiers. Brutus posts a guard outside his tent and he and Cassius remain inside.

COMMENT

Brutus is unhappy with Cassius, and their alliance is under strain.

Sardis the capital of the ancient kingdom of Lydia in what is now central Turkey, it was conquered by the Persians in 546BC

SCENE 3

Inside Brutus's tent

Cassius is angry with Brutus for having accused him of corruption. Brutus repeats the charge that Cassius has devalued their cause by selling official positions to undeserving people and suggests that Cassius is greedy. Cassius warns Brutus that if anyone else had said this, he would have killed him. Brutus reminds Cassius that they killed Caesar for the sake of justice and that they must not lose sight of the higher cause for which they acted. Cassius threatens Brutus who refuses to be intimidated. Brutus says that he will simply laugh at such foolish behaviour.

Cassius did not confront Caesar but plotted behind his back.

Cassius becomes angrier and says that even Caesar would not have dared to stand up to him. Brutus counters this by saying that Cassius would never have argued with Caesar. Brutus tells Cassius that he is annoyed with him because when he asked Cassius for gold to pay his army, Cassius refused him. Cassius tries to pass this off as a misunderstanding and blames the messenger. He then says that one friend should accept the other's faults. Cassius offers his dagger to Brutus and tells him to cut out his heart rather than to scorn him. Brutus tells Cassius to put away his dagger and the two men shake hands as friends.

A poet arrives to help the two generals resolve their quarrel. Brutus and Cassius laugh at him and send him away. Brutus now reveals that Portia is dead. Cassius marvels at the fact that Brutus did not kill him when they quarrelled earlier. Messala enters with news from Rome. He tells of many people killed on the orders of Antony, Octavius and Lepidus. He adds that Portia is dead, which Brutus already knows.

Brutus and Cassius discuss the approach of the armies of Antony and Octavius and decide to intercept them at

Philippi. Cassius is unhappy about this, but Brutus points out that the local people are unsympathetic and that if they do not fight soon their army, which is at its peak, can only decline. Cassius leaves and Brutus has Lucius play him some music. Varrus and Claudio (two servants of Brutus) lie down in his tent to guard him. Eventually, Brutus is the only one awake and the ghost of Caesar enters. The ghost tells him that they will meet again at Philippi. Brutus wakes the others and sends word to Cassius that their armies should prepare immediately for battle.

The ghost knows the future, rather like the soothsayer.

C OMMENT There is discord in the rebels' camp. This fits in with the notion that they have done something wrong, an important element in Elizabethan drama.

Portia has committed suicide at the news that Antony and Octavius have joined forces. Her death puts Brutus under even more pressure than before.

Messala brings news of Portia's death after Brutus has already told Cassius of it. Brutus takes the news of his wife's death, second time around, very calmly and so appears cold hearted. However, many scholars believe that this is a mistake made when the original stage text was first printed. They think that Shakespeare intended only one of the discussions of her death to be included.

Brutus takes a very philosophical view of life, comparing it to being afloat on a sea, pulled wherever the tide wishes.

Philippi was in Macedon, in what is now north-eastern Greece. It was, in fact, many hundreds of miles from Sardis, despite the impression given in the play.

Ghosts were very important to Elizabethans who believed that a ghost would appear after an unnatural death and torment the person responsible for it.

GLOSSARY

meet proper

mart trade, sell

bay howl at

testy humour irritable temper

rascal counters worthless pieces of metal

distract mad

Swallowed fire Plutarch says that Portia killed herself by putting hot coal in her mouth, then keeping it shut so that she choked

bound in shallows stuck in shallow water

How ill this taper burns Elizabethans believed that candle flames changed colour if a ghost appeared

betimes early

Identify the speaker.

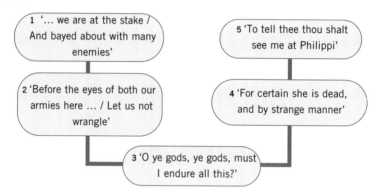

1 '... we are at the stake / And bayed about with many enemies'

5 'To tell thee thou shalt see me at Philippi'

2 'Before the eyes of both our armies here ... / Let us not wrangle'

4 'For certain she is dead, and by strange manner'

3 'O ye gods, ye gods, must I endure all this?'

Identify the person 'to whom' this comment refers.

6 'This is a slight, unmeritable man'

7 '... you yourself / Are much condemned to have an itching palm'

Check your answers on page 69.

Consider these issues.

a In Scene 1 Antony and Octavius argue and do not seem to be likely allies. Perhaps Antony feels he can manage without the help of Caesar's great-nephew.

b Could the discord between Brutus and Cassius indicate that their alliance is doomed?

c Why Brutus tries to pretend to be unaffected by the death of Portia.

d How much of his true nature Cassius reveals when he threatens Brutus, although he would never have challenged a great soldier such as Caesar.

e The role of the vengeful spirit in Elizabethan drama.

f To what extent vanity causes the downfall of great men in the play.

ACT V

SCENE 1

The battlefield at Philippi

Octavius and Antony have learnt that the armies of Brutus and Cassius have marched to Philippi to meet them. Octavius says that this has weakened the enemy's position as they have given up the high ground. Antony tells him that, by doing this, the enemy hope to appear brave, but that he is not fooled. Antony then tells Octavius to take the left-hand side of the battlefield but Octavius insists upon fighting on the right.

The opposing generals meet to exchange words before the battle begins. Antony rebukes Brutus for killing Caesar. He criticises the way they killed him while pretending to be his friends. Cassius tells Brutus that, had he been allowed to kill Antony, these insults would never have been uttered. Octavius swears to avenge the death of Caesar and leaves with Antony.

Eagles catch and kill their own prey; ravens, crows and kites eat carrion, feeding off human corpses and other dead things.

Cassius tells Messala of an omen he has seen: two eagles followed his army to Philippi and fed from the soldiers' hands, but that morning the eagles flew off and were replaced by ravens, crows and kites. Cassius and Brutus resolve not to allow themselves to be taken prisoner, though Brutus says that he will not commit suicide.

COMMENT

The right-hand side of the battlefield was considered to be the more honourable. The most important general fought on that side. In this argument Octavius is attempting to establish his superiority over Antony.

The eagle was an important symbol of power in Ancient Rome and was part of the standard of each legion.

Brutus and Cassius sound resigned to defeat, even though they each put on a brave face.

Remember, the ghost of Caesar has promised to be at
Philippi.

GLOSSARY   **fearful bravery** a show of courage designed to make the enemy
                afraid
                bloody sign of battle a red flag, the signal for battle
                exigent exigency, crisis
                Hybla a mountain in Sicily famous for its honey
                strain family
                As Pompey was Pompey was forced to fight at the battle of
                Pharsalus
                Epicurus (341–270BC) a Greek philosopher who believed
                that life on earth should be enjoyed to the full as all
                life ended in death; Epicurus would not have trusted
                omens
                led in triumph the Romans led their prisoners through the
                streets in front of jeering crowds

SCENE *2*   Brutus orders a messenger to tell the legions to
                   attack the army of Octavius. He thinks that the
The battlefield troops of Octavius look in low spirits and not ready to
at Philippi   fight.

COMMENT   At this stage of the battle Brutus is hopeful of
                   victory.

SCENE *3*   Cassius sees his soldiers fleeing from the battlefield. He
                   notes that Brutus gave the order to attack too early.
Philippi,   Pindarus, one of Cassius's servants, arrives and tells
overlooking   Cassius that Antony has entered his camp. Cassius asks
the battlefield his friend Titinius to ride to the camp to see whether
This misunder-   the troops there are friend or enemy. Pindarus watches
standing is fatal the progress of Titinius and reports that he has been
for Cassius.   taken prisoner. Cassius orders Pindarus to kill him with
                   the same sword that he himself used to assassinate
                   Caesar. Pindarus does so.

                   The scene then switches to another part of the
                   battlefield. Titinius has not been captured, he has met

Each man dies on the sword that helped kill Caesar.

Brutus's victorious army which has defeated Octavius. Messala and Titinius go to tell Cassius the good news but find him dead. Titinius places a victory wreath on the head of Cassius and then kills himself with Cassius's sword.

Brutus enters to find both Cassius and Titinius dead. He says that the spirit of Caesar is very powerful and has made his friends turn their swords upon themselves. Brutus orders the body of Cassius to be taken to Thasos. He then tells his men to prepare for a second battle, this time against Antony's army.

COMMENT   Titinius has not been captured but has met soldiers from Brutus's victorious army. Pindarus misinterprets what he sees far off and, as a result, Cassius kills himself.

Brutus comments about the power of Caesar's spirit. Certainly fate seems to have avenged his murder.

Brutus orders the body to be taken to Thasos, an island off the nearby coast, because holding the funeral in camp would lower his soldiers' morale.

GLOSSARY   ensign standard-bearer
on the spur spurring the horses on to run faster
darts envenomed poisoned arrows
set our battles on order our army to advance

SCENE 4

Another part of the battlefield

Cato and Lucilius are fighting soldiers from Antony's army. Cato is killed and Lucilius pretends to be Brutus. He admits the deception once Antony arrives. Antony tells his men to look after Lucilius and sets off to find Brutus.

COMMENT   Antony is impressed by the loyalty of Lucilius to Brutus.

SCENE 5   Brutus and his remaining friends stop to rest. He asks first Clitus then Dardanius to kill him. They refuse.

Elsewhere on Brutus says that he has seen the ghost of Caesar again
the battlefield and knows that it is time for him to die. Volumnius
refuses to accept this but Brutus says that he is defeated
The pit is a and has been driven 'to the pit'. He again asks the three
reference to a men to help him die, but again they refuse. Brutus is
grave and to Hell. left with his servant Strato, who was asleep during the
earlier conversation. Brutus asks Strato to hold his
sword and turn his face away while Brutus runs onto it.
Strato shakes Brutus's hand and agrees. Brutus runs
onto his own sword. His final words are that he killed
himself more willingly than he had killed Caesar.

Octavius and Antony enter with Messala and Lucilius.
Strato tells them how Brutus died and Octavius asks
the followers of Brutus to follow him now. Antony
comments that Brutus was 'the noblest Roman of them
all' and says that only Brutus killed Caesar out of a
sense of common good; all the others killed him out of
envy. Antony praises Brutus for his virtue. Octavius
says that Brutus will be given the funeral of a noble
soldier.

COMMENT   Although the Romans regarded suicide as noble, the
Elizabethans would have thought it dishonourable
as they believed that only God had the power to take
life.

Antony's remarks would please the followers of Brutus but not the friends of Cassius.

Antony and Octavius behave in a noble way, forgiving those who fought against them.

GLOSSARY   **showed the torch-light** Statilius showed a torch to indicate that only a few men had died

office task

smatch touch, small amount

the elements Brutus is said to have had the perfect balance of the elements (earth, fire, air and water). The Elizabethans believed that a person's character was determined by the proportion of each of the elements in it

TEST YOURSELF (Act V)

A Identify the speaker.

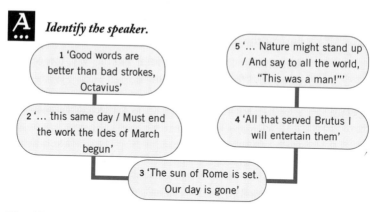

1 'Good words are better than bad strokes, Octavius'

5 '... Nature might stand up / And say to all the world, "This was a man!"'

2 '... this same day / Must end the work the Ides of March begun'

4 'All that served Brutus I will entertain them'

3 'The sun of Rome is set. Our day is gone'

Identify the person 'to whom' this comment refers.

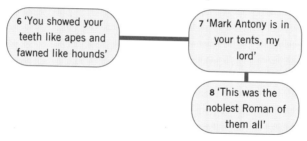

6 'You showed your teeth like apes and fawned like hounds'

7 'Mark Antony is in your tents, my lord'

8 'This was the noblest Roman of them all'

Check your answers on page 69.

B Consider these issues.

a Antony and Octavius argue virtually every time that we see them. Why is this significant historically as well as in the play?

b Octavius assumes he is Caesar's rightful heir. How far does this cause Antony to be resentful of him?

c Cassius and Brutus die like men, but only Brutus has the willpower to commit suicide. Why does Shakespeare stress this?

d How the tone of the play changes once the body of Brutus is found.

e To what degree does Antony regret the death of Brutus?

f By the end of the play the main conspirators are dead and Caesar's death has been avenged. Why would this have been important to an Elizabethan audience?

PART THREE

COMMENTARY

THEMES

POWER

The way that power affects the individual is an important theme. We see several major characters deal with the effects of power at various stages in the play.

When the play opens Caesar is the most powerful man in Rome. It is clear that he has been in positions of power for some time because he speaks quite comfortably about his own high status. There are, however, clear signs in his own speech that Caesar has begun to be affected by his power. He refers to himself in the third person, as 'Caesar', rather than in the first person, as 'I', suggesting that he has become rather full of his own importance. Some of the other characters speak of him as though he were a god. Antony says: 'When Caesar says "Do this", it is perform'd', a remark that shows that the commands of Caesar are law to many Romans.

Brutus behaves differently. He says he is not interested in power for himself. He is concerned that power should be exercised properly. In the context of the play this means by the Republic which had a system of elected government. In reality, the Republic was not democratic. Many of the conspirators acted against Caesar because they were frightened of losing the control of the Senate that their families had held for generations. Brutus is regarded as the senior member of the group that decides to kill Caesar and we see that Brutus does not use this power wisely. He overrules Cassius on three occasions, each with disastrous results. This shows that although Brutus has power he has neither the wisdom not the ruthlessness to use it

properly. While there seems little doubt that both
Caesar and Antony would have pursued their enemies,
Brutus forgives his. His motivation is honourable but
his opinion of Antony is a little naïve.

Mark Antony is a follower of Caesar in more ways
than one. After Caesar's death, Antony tries to act
as he thinks Caesar would have done and is prepared
to use his abilities to stir up the masses. Antony's
power over the people is similar to that of Caesar's,
as is his manipulation of the populace to serve his own
ends. Antony realises that he can be given power by
the people of Rome, whereas he is unable to seize
power by force. Once he has the power given by the
enraged masses he uses it ruthlessly to crush his
enemies. He makes better military decisions than
any of the other generals at Philippi, yet allows
Octavius to assume power. (Twelve years later
Antony was defeated by Octavius at the battle of
Actium.)

Octavius behaves as though it is natural for him to take
control in Rome following the death of Caesar.
Although he is supposedly in partnership with Antony
(and Lepidus), Octavius insists on taking the more
favourable side of the battlefield at Philippi. Antony lets
him, suggesting that Antony recognises the superiority
of Caesar's great-nephew. Shortly after the battle of
Philippi Octavius went to war against Antony and
eventually defeated him. Octavius took the name
Augustus and became the first Roman Emperor. He
certainly understood the nature of power.

LOYALTY

To the state   The murder of Caesar takes place for both personal and
public reasons, yet there are sufficient public reasons
alone for Brutus to join the conspiracy. Roman

noblemen were fiercely proud of their republican status and opposed a return to monarchy. The idea that the state encompassed everyone and acted in the common good was one that many senior Romans looked to as the example of good government. In reality, the government of Ancient Rome was little better than a dictatorship because ordinary people had no say in what was decided in their name. The important positions in Rome had been held by members of the same few families for years and so the notion of a people's republic was something of a sham.

All the actions in the play are carried out in the name of Rome. Each man adapts this notion of loyalty to the state to suit his own cause: Cassius to remove Caesar, of whom he is jealous; Antony to avenge his murdered friend.

Antony is loyal to the Rome that he knew under Caesar; a powerful nation made wealthy by conquest. Brutus is loyal to the notion of a republic, though was himself a member of a powerful and wealthy family.

It is no accident that all those characters who are disloyal to the state end up dead. This is because of the political climate when the play was written and first performed. A playwright dare not suggest that the murder of a king, or even a near king, would be allowed to go unpunished. Of course the events actually took place, but there is more than historical fact at work here. The conventions of Elizabethan England insisted that perpetrators of regicide (the murder of a king) should suffer.

To friends   The close personal relationships that exist between some of the characters are also factors in determining their actions. Antony acts largely out of a desire for personal revenge upon Caesar's killers. His close friendship is very important to him and is a major element of his motivation in pursuing Caesar's killers. Caesar had trusted Antony, as can be seen when he asked Antony to touch Calpurnia in the race at the festival of Lupercalia. The two men had fought many campaigns together and knew one another very well.

Brutus is friendly with Cassius and allows this friendship to cloud his judgement at times. Brutus is also aware of his own personal friendship with Caesar. Shakespeare is careful to observe the account of Caesar's death given by Plutarch in which Brutus strikes the fatal blow. This friendship affects Brutus greatly and he finds it difficult to overcome his feelings of personal grief at the death of Caesar.

Personal wishes are, however, seldom allowed to interfere with the larger issues at stake. The major characters in the play are all statesmen and understand, though to different degrees, the role of friendship and the use of power.

Within marriage

Two married couples appear in the play: Caesar and Calpurnia, and Brutus and Portia. The two relationships are in marked contrast. Caesar and Calpurnia seem to have a rather formal marriage. He is very much in charge, though he does show consideration for his wife's opinions when he decides to stay at home on the morning of the Ides of March. He is not relaxed enough with his wife to drop the habit of calling himself 'Caesar'. Perhaps this is intended to show his importance, but it does tend to make him appear a vain and inconsiderate husband.

Brutus and Portia, on the other hand, have a very close, trusting relationship. She goes to great lengths to prove her loyalty to her husband, wounding herself in the thigh and not complaining about it to prove she can bear great hardship when required to. He tells her of the plan to kill Caesar and this is the only example in the play of a man really letting a woman into his world. This marriage is much more of an equal partnership (at least in Elizabethan terms) than that between Caesar and Calpurnia.

STRUCTURE

The events of the play take place over three days. In real life this would not be possible, because it would have taken weeks for the armies to reach Philippi. On stage, however, the three-day model works very effectively. Each day is neatly split into sections from morning until night, as follows:

Day one In the morning the people take to the streets to praise Caesar.

In the afternoon the games of the Lupercalia festival are held and Cassius approaches Brutus about joining the conspiracy.

At night there are terrible storms as the conspirators discuss the plot at Brutus's house.

Day two In the morning Calpurnia tells Caesar of her dream. He then goes to the Senate with the conspirators and is killed shortly afterwards.

In the afternoon Antony stirs up the crowd against the conspirators at Caesar's funeral.

In the evening Octavius, Lepidus and Antony meet. Brutus and Cassius argue then reconcile their differences.

Day three In the morning the generals meet.

In the afternoon the battle begins.

In the evening Cassius commits suicide and Brutus kills himself that night.

Although nonsense in terms of the real passage of time, by reducing the action to three days, Shakespeare gives the audience a clearly defined time frame, so making the action seem more realistic. It also adds to the urgency and dramatic tension of the play as matters have to be resolved in such a short time.

CHARACTERS

JULIUS CAESAR

Ruthless
Powerful
Ambitious
Manipulative
Vain

The Caesar that we see at the opening of the play is the greatest and most powerful man in Rome. He has defeated Pompey, his closest rival, and has effectively taken charge of the empire. The only thing he lacks is the crown. Caesar is ambitious, yet he can also be very human. His first concern in the play is that Antony, when running in the race at the festival of the Lupercalia, should touch Calpurnia so that she might conceive a child. He appears here to be a considerate man, affected by the same everyday concerns as anyone else. However this concern could also be interpreted as vanity: he is ageing (see below) and has no heir, so would appear still young and virile if his wife became pregnant.

We hear from Cassius that Caesar has started to behave as if he were a god. This might simply be jealousy on the part of Cassius, a man whom Caesar did not favour. But there must be some truth in it because Brutus becomes involved in the conspiracy.

Caesar is clearly ambitious and Casca's amusing account of the scene at the Lupercalia games, where Caesar refused the crown when he obviously wanted to accept it, shows us this. He speaks of himself as being different to ordinary men, telling Metellus that he, Caesar, does not act unjustly and cannot be swayed as

other men might be. This suggests a certain arrogance
on his part. It is clear in this scene (Act III, Scene 1)
why some men feel aggrieved at Caesar's self-
importance. His constant references to himself in the
third person add to this impression.

Caesar's vanity is clear when he decides to go to the
Capitol in order to avoid being laughed at. This is
another side of Caesar which shows weakness. He is far
from the invincible, god-like creature he wishes to
appear. Caesar has physical weaknesses too: his
epilepsy, fevers and partial deafness show him to be
more frail than he would have people think.
Shakespeare has chosen to portray Caesar as an ageing
man. This certainly makes him more human and more
believable.

MARCUS BRUTUS

Marcus Brutus is widely regarded as a noble man. He is
a friend of Caesar and is forced to examine his
conscience closely over the assassination of a man he
loves and respects. Brutus is something of an idealist.
He believes in the Republic as the best form of
government. Because of his love for Rome he allows
himself to be drawn into the plot to kill Caesar. Antony
remarks that Brutus was the only one of the group who
did not kill Caesar because of envy and personal
grievance. Brutus acted in what he thought were the
best interests of Rome.

Honourable
Idealistic
Courageous
Loving
Trusting

Brutus proves himself to be a poor judge of character as
he places too much trust in Cassius. He is flattered by
the words that apparently came from anonymous
citizens and so shows that, like Caesar, he can be vain.
Though he believes what Cassius later tells him, Brutus
does not allow the murder of Caesar to become a
massacre of his supporters too. He restrains Cassius

and the others, even over the fate of Mark Antony. This proves fatal.

Of all the men in the play, Brutus is the only one whose domestic life we see much of. His very close relationship with Portia is in contrast to the more formal one between Caesar and Calpurnia. Brutus shows his courage when accepting the news of Portia's death. This courage also manifests itself in his suicide when all is lost at Philippi. He dies in a manner that Romans would have thought brave and avoids the humiliation of being led through the streets of Rome as a prisoner.

Brutus lets his idealism overcome his reason and pays the price for it.

CASSIUS

At the start of the play Cassius is a mean man, consumed by jealousy. He resents the fact that Caesar shows him no favour and is clearly envious of Caesar's growing power and popularity. There is little in him to make the audience feel sympathy for his cause.

Cassius is easily excited, yet proves to be a better judge of character and of strategy than the more placid Brutus. Cassius plots Caesar's murder and is responsible for recruiting the conspirators. The judgements of Cassius regarding the killing of Antony and the fighting of a battle at Philippi prove to be more sound than those of Brutus. Even so, he takes unnecessary risks, such as walking the streets during the storm, tempting the lightning to strike him.

Jealous
Scheming
Impulsive
Good strategist
Quick tempered

As the play develops, and particularly after the death of Caesar, Cassius becomes a more sympathetic character. At Philippi he is able to console Brutus over the death of Portia. His friendship with Brutus redeems him as a

man and causes the audience to warm to him. His
death is tragic as it occurs because of his hot-
headedness. He is a complex character, capable of the
full range of human emotions.

MARK ANTONY

Until the death of Caesar, Antony is little more than a
follower. He is a friend to Caesar, in much the same
way that Cassius is to Brutus. Antony has been a
successful soldier and is underestimated by Brutus. His
character becomes really defined when he gives the
stirring oration over Caesar's body, and shows a new
side of himself. He is a skilful orator and easily turns
the crowd to his way of thinking. He shows that he has
a logical mind and that he can be ruthless when in
pursuit of the enemy.

Ruthless
Loyal
Shrewd
Emotional
Calculating

This ruthless side comes to the fore when he is trading
the lives of the traitors for his own political ends. The
death of Caesar, his beloved friend, brings out
characteristics in Antony which he has doubtless used
before in battle, but which we did not see in the first
half of the play. The chillingly calculating avenger
emerges from the funeral of Caesar and he proves
himself to be a powerful statesman. Interestingly, he
allows Octavius to overrule him at Philippi, though this
is possibly due to loyalty to Julius Caesar who had
appointed Octavius his heir. Antony is also shrewd
enough to avoid a split in the Roman forces just before
a major battle. Although he takes the inferior side of
the battlefield he is victorious, whereas Octavius is
defeated.

Antony is driven by his emotions and will not allow
anything or anyone to stand in the way of what he feels
to be right. In this way he could be said to be similar to
Brutus. Antony has a savage streak which Brutus lacks

and it is this savagery which leads him to victory and ensures that he avenges Caesar's murder. Antony proves himself to be a great leader of men, a powerful public speaker and a cunning politician.

MINOR CHARACTERS

CALPURNIA

Calpurnia is a level-headed woman who does not normally let herself be influenced by superstition. She shows her affection for her husband on the morning of the Ides of March when she attempts to prevent him going to the Capitol. Calpurnia is intelligent and recognises that Caesar has become overconfident. She is worried by her dream, but also by the fact that Caesar seems to be beginning to believe that he is invincible. She does not seem to have any ambition for herself and does not show any sign of being impressed by Caesar's imminent promotion to king.

PORTIA

Portia is portrayed as a good Roman wife. She is loyal and caring towards Brutus and would clearly go to any lengths to protect him. She is a passionate woman as shown by her action to prove she can keep a secret. Wounding herself in the thigh is a drastic act, but is very much the behaviour of someone who can easily allow passion to overrule reason. She is a good contrast to the colder Brutus.

Ultimately it is this passion and loyalty which are her undoing. Unable to contemplate life without Brutus, she swallows hot coals and dies in a typically tragic manner.

CASCA

Casca is a cynical man; he is in fact a Cynic. Followers of this school of Greek philosophy believed that virtue is the only good and that it can only be achieved by individual self-control, and not by imposed social conventions. The account he gives of the Lupercalia games is humorous and dry. He has little time for pretence and is very cutting in his remarks about Caesar's behaviour. He is referred to as a 'plain blunt man' and shows little emotion when first we meet him. However, Casca is not as impervious to superstition as he would like us to believe. He is terrified by the storm and becomes excited when recounting the strange things he has seen.

DECIUS BRUTUS

It is Decius who raises the question of killing Caesar's followers as well as Caesar himself. He is also the man who flatters Caesar sufficiently to bring him to the Capitol. Decius is a skilful and persuasive speaker. He obviously knows Caesar's weaknesses and is intelligent enough to use them to get what he wants. Decius expects Caesar to accompany him to the Capitol rather than let himself be laughed at. This shows a certain shrewdness in his nature.

OCTAVIUS CAESAR

Octavius is the heir to Julius Caesar's wealth and position. He is the great-nephew of Julius Caesar and regards himself as successor to power in Rome. He is not as good a general as Antony, but still insists on ordering the battle lines at Philippi. His character is not clearly defined but he shows something of the nature that will enable him to become Augustus Caesar. He is clear in his own mind and will not budge once he has made a decision. This is a potential weakness, yet he shows many of Julius Caesar's qualities when dealing with people.

LANGUAGE & STYLE

Julius Caesar contains powerful and striking language. The Elizabethan view of Ancient Rome as a place of great nobility and honour is reflected in the speech of the characters in the play. Shakespeare makes great use of rich imagery (see Literary Terms) to create the world of Rome on the stage. The play is full of references to the buildings and statues of Rome, creating an impression of a place which is cultured and powerful.

Two types of language are used in the play: blank verse and prose (see Literary Terms). In Shakespeare's plays it is usually the lower-class characters who speak in prose. Important and noble characters tend to speak in blank verse. Interestingly, the funeral speech made by Brutus is in prose, perhaps to signify his wish to communicate with ordinary people. In contrast, when Antony speaks to the crowd in his famous 'Friends, Romans, countrymen' speech he uses verse. Antony's speech is full of high poetry, for example, 'O judgement, thou art fled to brutish beasts, / And men have lost their reason.'

He makes self-contained statements about the greatness, kindness and honour of Caesar and then adds that the conspirators are 'honourable men'. This use of reasoned argument is known as rhetoric (see Literary Terms). Elizabethan schoolchildren studied rhetoric and it was considered a good way of demonstrating how clever (witty) you were.

Prose is used by Casca when he gives his account of Caesar's refusal to take the crown at the games. This use of informal language allows the character to develop the humour of the situation. It also tells the audience that Casca does not take Caesar seriously.

One other notable use of language is in the way Julius Caesar refers to himself in the third person. He calls himself 'Caesar' instead of 'I'. Even when speaking to his wife he says 'Caesar shall forth'. This has two effects: it distances Caesar from the rest of the characters and makes him sound rather pompous and self-important.

It is the blend of rich imagery and dramatic expression which gives the language of *Julius Caesar* its power.

PART FOUR

Study Skills

How to use quotations

One of the secrets of success in writing essays is the way you use quotations. There are five basic principles:

- Put inverted commas at the beginning and end of the quotation
- Write the quotation exactly as it appears in the original
- Do not use a quotation that repeats what you have just written
- Use the quotation so that it fits into your sentence
- Keep the quotation as short as possible

Quotations should be used to develop the line of thought in your essays.

Your comment should not duplicate what is in your quotation. For example:

> Antony says that his heart is in the coffin with Caesar: 'My heart is in the coffin there with Caesar'

Far more effective is to write:

> Antony shows the crowd how much he has been hurt by Caesar's death: 'My heart is in the coffin there with Caesar'

Always lay out the lines as they appear in the text. For example:

> '... Danger knows full well
> That Caesar is more dangerous than he:'

However, the most sophisticated way of using the writer's words is to embed them into your sentence:

> Cassius says that he has seen the mighty Caesar cry 'as a sick girl' and reminds Brutus that 'this god did shake' when he had a fever.

When you use quotations in this way, you are demonstrating the ability to use text as evidence to support your ideas - not simply including words from the original to prove you have read it.

Everyone writes differently. Work through the suggestions given here and adapt the advice to suit your own style and interests. This will improve your essay-writing skills and allow your personal voice to emerge.

The following points indicate in ascending order the skills of essay writing:

- Picking out one or two facts about the story and adding the odd detail
- Writing about the text by retelling the story
- Retelling the story and adding a quotation here and there
- Organising an answer which explains what is happening in the text and giving quotations to support what you write

....

- Writing in such a way as to show that you have thought about the intentions of the writer of the text and that you understand the techniques used
- Writing at some length, giving your viewpoint on the text and commenting by picking out details to support your views
- Looking at the text as a work of art, demonstrating clear critical judgement and explaining to the reader of your essay how the enjoyment of the text is assisted by literary devices, linguistic effects and psychological insights; showing how the text relates to the time when it was written

The dotted line above represents the division between lower and higher level grades. Higher-level performance begins when you start to consider your response as a reader of the text. The highest level is reached when you offer an enthusiastic personal response and show how this piece of literature is a product of its time.

Coursework essay

Set aside an hour or so at the start of your work to plan what you have to do.

- List all the points you feel are needed to cover the task. Collect page references of information and quotations that will support what you have to say. A helpful tool is the highlighter pen: this saves painstaking copying and enables you to target precisely what you want to use.
- Focus on what you consider to be the main points of the essay. Try to sum up your argument in a single sentence, which could be the closing sentence of your essay. Depending on the essay title, it could be a statement about a character: Brutus is a noble man. He feels that he is acting in the best interests of the people of Rome; an opinion about setting: It is quite fitting that the conspirators meet at the statue of Pompey to discuss the murder of Caesar; or a judgement on a theme: The effects of power upon the individual is an important theme in the play.
- Make a short essay plan. Use the first paragraph to introduce the argument you wish to make. In the following paragraphs develop this argument with details, examples and other possible points of view. Sum up your argument in the last paragraph. Check you have answered the question.
- Write the essay, remembering all the time the central point you are making.
- On completion, go back over what you have written to eliminate careless errors and improve expression. Read it aloud to yourself, or, if you are feeling more confident, to a relative or friend.

If you can, try to type your essay, using a word processor. This will allow you to correct and improve your writing without spoiling its appearance.

Examination essay

The essay written in an examination often carries more marks than the coursework essay even though it is written under considerable time pressure.

In the revision period build up notes on various aspects of the text you are using. Fortunately, in acquiring this set of York Notes on *Julius Caesar*, you have made a prudent beginning! York Notes are set out to give you vital information and help you to construct your personal overview of the text.

Make notes with appropriate quotations about the key issues of the set text. Go into the examination knowing your text and having a clear set of opinions about it.

In most English Literature examinations you can take in copies of your set books. This in an enormous advantage although it may lull you into a false sense of security. Beware! There is simply not enough time in an examination to read the book from scratch.

In the examination

- Read the question paper carefully and remind yourself what you have to do.
- Look at the questions on your set texts to select the one that most interests you and mentally work out the points you wish to stress.
- Remind yourself of the time available and how you are going to use it.
- Briefly map out a short plan in note form that will keep your writing on track and illustrate the key argument you want to make.
- Then set about writing it.
- When you have finished, check through to eliminate errors.

To summarise, these are the keys to success:

- **Know the text**
- **Have a clear understanding of and opinions on the storyline, characters, setting, themes and writer's concerns**
- **Select the right material**
- **Plan and write a clear response, continually bearing the question in mind**

SAMPLE ESSAY PLAN

A typical essay question on *Julius Caesar* is followed by a sample essay plan in note form. This does not present the only answer to the question, merely one answer. Do not be afraid to include your own ideas and leave out some of the ones in this sample! Remember that quotations are essential to prove and illustrate the points you make.

Say how far you think Caesar contributes to his own downfall.

The essay needs an introduction, main argument and conclusion. It is better to take a balanced view than to launch into a one-sided answer. The argument might be set out as follows.

Introduction Refer to the definition of tragedy (see Literary Terms) as a fall from greatness due to a flaw in character. If this is the case for Caesar he must have a flaw. In fact there are two major flaws in Caesar's nature: his ambition and his vanity, but he has strengths too.

Part 1 Discuss the strengths of Caesar. He has many strengths. One of the most important is his sense of public duty. Caesar treats the citizens well, as can be seen by their reaction in the opening scene. We see Caesar's human side at his first entrance: he wants Antony to touch Calpurnia in the race so that she might conceive a child. We see his strength of will when he dismisses the soothsayer as 'a dreamer'.

Caesar shows that he can be a good judge of character when he makes comments about Cassius. He also seems sure that Antony is loyal and trusts him enough to ask him to touch Calpurnia in the Lupercalia race. This shows that Caesar has faith in Antony (but also that he is desperate for an heir).

At the games Caesar's shameless manipulation of the crowd shows how shrewd he is. He knows what the people want to see and how to provide it.

We do not see Caesar the soldier in the play but his reputation as both a great general and a great fighter is referred to on several occasions.

On the way to the Capitol Caesar is stopped by Artemidorus. He shows another side here when refusing to read the petition of Artemidorus. He is told the petition concerns himself and so he says he will read it last. (Ironically, this public humility, whether real or sham, helps bring about his death.) There are signs here of the Caesar who was loved by the ordinary people of Rome.

Part 2   Now turn to the weaknesses of Caesar. Casca reports that Caesar could hardly bring himself to refuse the crown when it was offered to him at the games. There are clear signs here of the ambition of Caesar: he is not going to refuse the crown if it is offered to him again.

When Caesar next appears we see some signs of his vanity. He says his name is not 'liable to fear'. He then refers to himself as 'Caesar' for the first time. This might indicate foolish pride. Certainly he feels he is invulnerable.

Calpurnia succeeds in dissuading Caesar from going to the Capitol. It is his ambition and vanity which overcome his reason when Decius says that Calpurnia's dream is a good sign and that people will laugh at Caesar for doing what his wife tells him.

Caesar relaxes when surrounded by the conspirators and could be said to be either too trusting or too convinced that no one would dare to attack him to take precautions.

Conclusion   Caesar's ambition and vanity certainly contributed to his downfall. So too did his sense of public duty. This contradiction makes the character of Caesar and the play fascinating. There are certainly flaws in the character of Caesar and so the traditions of tragedy are observed.

Make a plan as shown and attempt these quaestions.

1 In what ways could Julius Caesar be said to be a great statesman?

2 On three separate occasions Brutus ignores advice from Cassius. Say what these occasions are and:
   a) why Brutus ignores the advice and
   b) what the consequences are.

3 Julius Caesar dies less than halfway through the play. Explain how Shakespeare maintains the audience's interest once Caesar is dead.

4 Brutus is a man torn between personal loyalty and public duty. Discuss the dilemma he faces over the murder of Caesar and say why you think he arrives at the decision he does.

5 Say how Shakespeare deals with power in *Julius Caesar*.

6 Discuss the portrayal of the relationship between
   a) Caesar and Calpurnia
   b) Brutus and Portia
and show how far each man is influenced by his wife.

7 Discuss the character of Cassius and say how far your opinion of him has changed by the end of the play.

8 The supernatural plays an important part in *Julius Caesar*. Discuss the different ways in which the supernatural features in the play.

9 Is it inevitable that Brutus and Cassius die for their parts in the murder of Caesar?

10 Discuss Shakespeare's portrayal of Antony. Make particular reference to the funeral orations.

PART FIVE

CULTURAL CONNECTIONS

BROADER PERSPECTIVES

Books

There are many books on the subject of Ancient Rome. Every good encyclopedia contains a wealth of information about Rome and its most famous figures. Among the fiction that sheds some light on the time you will find:

I Claudius and *Claudius the God* by Robert Graves

These historical novels deal with the political intrigue of life in Roman society and expose the corruption found even at the highest levels of life. Available in paperback. They were made into a famous BBC television series, *I Claudius*, in 1976.

Alan Massie has written several novels set in Ancient Rome. *Tiberius* deals with many of the same problems that appear in Shakespeare's *Julius Caesar* and *Antony* focuses on Mark Antony.

Some background reading on the myths and legends of the ancient world would also be useful to give an idea of the beliefs of the people of that time. *Men and Gods* by Rex Warner is a collection of such tales.

Extracts from Caesar's own *Commentaries* on the Gallic Wars can be found in many collections of writing from Ancient Rome.

Films

Ancient Rome has inspired many films. Epics such as *Spartacus*, *Cleopatra* and *Ben Hur* are lavish productions and show something of the spectacle of Rome. The 1953 film version of *Julius Caesar*, starring Marlon Brando and James Mason, is true to Shakespeare's text.

The Monty Python team gave their own rendering of the Roman occupation of Judea at the time of Christ in *The Life of Brian*, though this should not be taken as real history.

aside words spoken by a character in a play which some (or all) of the other characters on stage do not hear. Asides are often addressed directly to the audience and indicate the character's thoughts and feelings

blank verse lines which have rhythm or metre, but do not rhyme. Most of this play is in blank verse, with iambic pentameters as the type of verse used

dramatic irony when the audience knows more about events in the play than the characters concerned, or what will happen as a result of one of the character's actions, for example, when Caesar unsuspectingly tells Trebonius (one of the conspirators) to draw close just before the assassins strike

figure of speech describing something in a more vivid or colourful way than is strictly necessary

heroic couplet two lines of iambic pentameter that rhyme. Shakespeare often uses an heroic couplet to mark the end of a scene (there were no stage curtains in the Elizabethan theatre) or to announce something very important

iambic pentameter a form of poetry in which the lines consist of five pairs of syllables, the first syllable is unstressed and is followed by one that is stressed; most of the speeches in this play are in iambic pentameter

imagery word pictures which help the audience (or reader) understand or interpret different events, for example, Brutus's description of his army's standards before the battle

irony/ironic saying (or writing) one thing, but meaning another, usually the opposite of what has been said

metre another word for rhythm; although there are many different types of rhythm each one is simply a different arrangement of stressed and unstressed syllables

oration a formal speech made at a solemn public occasion, such as a funeral

prose what we would call 'ordinary speech', prose has no set pattern of rhythm. Characters speak in prose in Shakespeare's plays either because the person speaking is unimportant or the conversation is between people who know each other well and feel relaxed together. Prose is much less formal than verse. Compare the funeral oration given by Brutus, which is in prose, and Antony's which is in blank verse

pun a play on words; using a word that has two very different meanings. The Elizabethans were very fond of puns and considered that someone who could pun well was intelligent

rhetoric the art of speaking effectively and persuading an audience to accept your point of view, as Antony persuaded the people of Rome to turn against Caesar's murderers

soliloquy a speech made by a character directly to the audience which reveals his or her thoughts

tragedy a drama which traces the career and downfall of one of the characters due to a flaw in his or her character; Brutus says that ambition is Caesar's fatal flaw. In a tragedy the tragic hero or heroine brings about his or her own downfall

TEST ANSWERS

TEST YOURSELF (Act I)

A 1 Caesar *(I.2.7–8)*
··· 2 Brutus *(I.2.28–9)*
3 Cassius *(I.2.135–6)*
4 Brutus *(I.2.284)*
5 Casca *(I.3.85–6)*
6 Caesar *(I.2.119–21)*
7 Cassius *(I.2.202–3)*
8 Brutus *(I.2.298–9)*

TEST YOURSELF (Act II)

A 1 Brutus *(II.1.22)*
··· 2 Cassius *(II.1.222–3)*
3 Calpurnia *(II.2.25–6)*
4 Portia *(II.3.7)*
5 Artemidorus *(II.3.1)*
6 Caesar *(II.1.20)*
7 Cicero *(II.1.144–5)*
8 Caesar *(II.2.38)*

TEST YOURSELF (Act III)

A 1 Popillius *(III.1.13)*
··· 2 Cinna *(III.1.78)*
3 Antony *(III.1.148)*
4 Brutus *(III.2.13)*

5 Antony *(III.2.66)*
6 Metellus *(III.1.46)*
7 Brutus *(III.1.138)*
8 The people of Rome
(III.2.160)

TEST YOURSELF (Act IV)

A 1 Octavius *(IV.1.48–9)*
··· 2 Brutus *(IV.2.43–5)*
3 Cassius *(IV.3.41)*
4 Messala *(IV.3.189)*
5 Caesar's ghost *(IV.3.283)*
6 Lepidus *(IV.1.11)*
7 Cassius *(IV.3.9–10)*

TEST YOURSELF (Act V)

A 1 Brutus *(V.1.29)*
··· 2 Brutus *(V.1.112)*
3 Titinius *(V.3.63)*
4 Octavius *(V.5.60)*
5 Antony *(V.5.75)*
6 Brutus, Cassius and the
conspirators *(V.1.41)*
7 Cassius *(V.3.10)*
8 Brutus *(V.5.68)*

NOTES

NOTES

NOTES

NOTES

NOTES

GCSE and equivalent levels (£3.50 each)

Maya Angelou
I Know Why the Caged Bird Sings

Jane Austen
Pride and Prejudice

Harold Brighouse
Hobson's Choice

Charlotte Brontë
Jane Eyre

Emily Brontë
Wuthering Heights

Charles Dickens
David Copperfield

Charles Dickens
Great Expectations

Charles Dickens
Hard Times

George Eliot
Silas Marner

William Golding
Lord of the Flies

Willis Hall
The Long and the Short and the Tall

Thomas Hardy
Far from the Madding Crowd

Thomas Hardy
The Mayor of Casterbridge

Thomas Hardy
Tess of the d'Urbervilles

L.P. Hartley
The Go-Between

Seamus Heaney
Selected Poems

Susan Hill
I'm the King of the Castle

Barry Hines
A Kestrel for a Knave

Louise Lawrence
Children of the Dust

Harper Lee
To Kill a Mockingbird

Laurie Lee
Cider with Rosie

Arthur Miller
A View from the Bridge

Arthur Miller
The Crucible

Robert O'Brien
Z for Zachariah

George Orwell
Animal Farm

J.B. Priestley
An Inspector Calls

Willy Russell
Educating Rita

Willy Russell
Our Day Out

J.D. Salinger
The Catcher in the Rye

William Shakespeare
Henry V

William Shakespeare
Julius Caesar

William Shakespeare
Macbeth

William Shakespeare
A Midsummer Night's Dream

William Shakespeare
The Merchant of Venice

William Shakespeare
Romeo and Juliet

William Shakespeare
The Tempest

William Shakespeare
Twelfth Night

George Bernard Shaw
Pygmalion

R.C. Sherriff
Journey's End

Rukshana Smith
Salt on the snow

John Steinbeck
Of Mice and Men

R.L. Stevenson
Dr Jekyll and Mr Hyde

Robert Swindells
Daz 4 Zoe

Mildred D. Taylor
Roll of Thunder, Hear My Cry

Mark Twain
The Adventures of Huckleberry Finn

James Watson
Talking in Whispers

A Choice of Poets

Nineteenth Century Short Stories

Poetry of the First World War

Six Women Poets

Advanced level (£3.99 each)

Margaret Atwood
The Handmaid's Tale

William Blake
Songs of Innocence and of Experience

Emily Brontë
Wuthering Heights

Geoffrey Chaucer
The Wife of Bath's Prologue and Tale

Joseph Conrad
Heart of Darkness

Charles Dickens
Great Expectations

F. Scott Fitzgerald
The Great Gatsby

Thomas Hardy
Tess of the d'Urbervilles

James Joyce
Dubliners

Arthur Miller
Death of a Salesman

William Shakespeare
Antony and Cleopatra

William Shakespeare
Hamlet

William Shakespeare
King Lear

William Shakespeare
The Merchant of Venice

William Shakespeare
Romeo and Juliet

William Shakespeare
The Tempest

Mary Shelley
Frankenstein

Alice Walker
The Color Purple

Tennessee Williams
A Streetcar Named Desire

Jane Austen
Emma

Jane Austen
Pride and Prejudice

Charlotte Brontë
Jane Eyre

Seamus Heaney
Selected Poems

William Shakespeare
Much Ado About Nothing

William Shakespeare
Othello

John Webster
The Duchess of Malfi

FUTURE TITLES IN THE YORK NOTES SERIES

Chinua Achebe
Things Fall Apart

Edward Albee
Who's Afraid of Virginia Woolf?

Jane Austen
Mansfield Park

Jane Austen
Northanger Abbey

Jane Austen
Persuasion

Jane Austen
Sense and Sensibility

Samuel Beckett
Waiting for Godot

Alan Bennett
Talking Heads

John Betjeman
Selected Poems

Robert Bolt
A Man for All Seasons

Robert Burns
Selected Poems

Lord Byron
Selected Poems

Geoffrey Chaucer
The Franklin's Tale

Geoffrey Chaucer
The Merchant's Tale

Geoffrey Chaucer
The Miller's Tale

Geoffrey Chaucer
The Nun's Priest's Tale

Geoffrey Chaucer
Prologue to the Canterbury Tales

Samuel Taylor Coleridge
Selected Poems

Daniel Defoe
Moll Flanders

Daniel Defoe
Robinson Crusoe

Shelagh Delaney
A Taste of Honey

Charles Dickens
Bleak House

Charles Dickens
Oliver Twist

Emily Dickinson
Selected Poems

John Donne
Selected Poems

Douglas Dunn
Selected Poems

George Eliot
Middlemarch

George Eliot
The Mill on the Floss

T.S. Eliot
The Waste Land

T.S. Eliot
Selected Poems

Henry Fielding
Joseph Andrews

E.M. Forster
Howards End

E.M. Forster
A Passage to India

John Fowles
The French Lieutenant's Woman

Brian Friel
Translations

Elizabeth Gaskell
North and South

Oliver Goldsmith
She Stoops to Conquer

Graham Greene
Brighton Rock

Thomas Hardy
Jude the Obscure

Thomas Hardy
Selected Poems

Nathaniel Hawthorne
The Scarlet Letter

Ernest Hemingway
The Old Man and the Sea

Homer
The Iliad

Homer
The Odyssey

Aldous Huxley
Brave New World

Ben Jonson
The Alchemist

Ben Jonson
Volpone

James Joyce
A Portrait of the Artist as a Young Man

John Keats
Selected Poems

Philip Larkin
Selected Poems

D.H. Lawrence
The Rainbow

D.H. Lawrence
Sons and Lovers

D.H. Lawrence
Women in Love

Christopher Marlowe
Doctor Faustus

John Milton
Paradise Lost Bks I & II

John Milton
Paradise Lost IV & IX

Sean O'Casey
Juno and the Paycock

George Orwell
Nineteen Eighty-four

John Osborne
Look Back in Anger

Wilfred Owen
Selected Poems

Harold Pinter
The Caretaker

Sylvia Plath
Selected Works

Alexander Pope
Selected Poems

Jean Rhys
Wide Sargasso Sea

William Shakespeare
As You Like It

William Shakespeare
Coriolanus

William Shakespeare
Henry IV Pt 1

William Shakespeare
Henry V

William Shakespeare
Julius Caesar

William Shakespeare
Measure for Measure

William Shakespeare
Much Ado About Nothing

William Shakespeare
A Midsummer Night's Dream

William Shakespeare
Richard II

William Shakespeare
Richard III

William Shakespeare
Sonnets

William Shakespeare
The Taming of the Shrew

William Shakespeare
The Winter's Tale

George Bernard Shaw
Arms and the Man

George Bernard Shaw
Saint Joan

Richard Brinsley Sheridan
The Rivals

Muriel Spark
The Prime of Miss Jean Brodie

John Steinbeck
The Grapes of Wrath

John Steinbeck
The Pearl

Tom Stoppard
Rosencrantz and Guildenstern are Dead

Jonathan Swift
Gulliver's Travels

John Millington Synge
The Playboy of the Western World

W.M. Thackeray
Vanity Fair

Virgil
The Aeneid

Derek Walcott
Selected Poems

Oscar Wilde
The Importance of Being Earnest

Tennessee Williams
Cat on a Hot Tin Roof

Tennessee Williams
The Glass Menagerie

Virginia Woolf
Mrs Dalloway

Virginia Woolf
To the Lighthouse

William Wordsworth
Selected Poems

W.B. Yeats
Selected Poems

York Notes – the Ultimate Literature Guides

York Notes are recognised as the best literature study guides.
If you have enjoyed using this book and have found it useful, you
can now order others directly from us – simply follow the ordering
instructions below.

HOW TO ORDER

Decide which title(s) you require and then order in one of the following
ways:

Booksellers
All titles available from good bookstores.

By post
List the title(s) you require in the space provided overleaf,
select your method of payment, complete your name and
address details and return your completed order form and
payment to:

> *Addison Wesley Longman Ltd*
> *PO BOX 88*
> *Harlow*
> *Essex CM19 5SR*

By phone
Call our Customer Information Centre on 01279 623923 to
place your order, quoting mail number: HEYN1.

By fax
Complete the order form overleaf, ensuring you fill in your
name and address details and method of payment, and fax it
to us on 01279 414130.

By e-mail
E-mail your order to us on awlhe.orders@awl.co.uk listing
title(s) and quantity required and providing full name and
address details as requested overleaf. Please quote mail
number: HEYN1. Please do not send credit card details by
e-mail.

York Notes Order Form

Titles required:

Quantity	Title/ISBN	Price

Sub total _____

Please add £2.50 postage & packing _____

(*P & P is free for orders over £50*) _____

Total _____

Mail no: HEYN1

Your Name _____

Your Address _____

Postcode _____ Telephone _____

Method of payment

☐ I enclose a cheque or a P/O for £_____ made payable to Addison Wesley Longman Ltd

☐ Please charge my Visa/Access/AMEX/Diners Club card
Number _____ Expiry Date _____
Signature _____ Date _____

(please ensure that the address given above is the same as for your credit card)

Prices and other details are correct at time of going to press but may change without notice. All orders are subject to status.

☐ *Please tick this box if you would like a complete listing of Longman Study Guides (suitable for GCSE and A-level students)*

⊚ York Press

📖 Longman

Addison Wesley Longman